AF100625

The Dad-A-Base

You go to Source for Pun-tastic, eye-rolling, grown worthy jokes for the whole family

Dr. Scott

Copyright © 2024

All Rights Reserved

ISBN:

Dedication

To my beloved son Beckham, and every child that is impacted by separation and divorce....

May this book serve as a constant companion on those long car rides, when boredom strikes and time seems to stretch like taffy. Let these pages be a reminder of our shared laughter, and a testament to the joys hidden within life's traffic jams. Remember, my son, that just like a stubborn GPS, I'll always be here to recalculate and guide you, even when you take an unexpected exit or two. In the grand road trip of life, know that my love comes from God through me to you and is the ultimate fuel. Unlimited and premium grade. So, buckle up, enjoy the ride, and never forget: Your old men got your back, come smooth highways or pot-

holed streets. With all my love and a tank full of dad jokes,

Dad

P.S. If you're reading this while driving, pull over immediately!

Safety first, son. Safety first.

Contents

Dedication ii

Knock Knock Non-Sense 1

Sports 21

Animal Antics 38

Food 48

Pun-tastic Puns 57

Miscellaneous Mischief 63

Page Blank Intentionally

Knock Knock

Non-Sense

1. Knock Knock.
Who's there?
Lettuce.
Lettuce who?
Lettuce in, it's cold out here!

2. Knock Knock.
Who's there?
Interrupting cow.
Interrupting cow w- MOO!

3. Knock Knock.
Who's there?
Broken pencil.
Broken pencil who?
Never mind, it's pointless.

4. Knock Knock.
Who's there?
Boo.
Boo who?
Don't cry, it's just a joke!

5. Knock Knock.
Who's there?
Cows go.
Cows go who?
No, silly, cows go "moo"!

6. Knock Knock.
Who's there?
Banana.
Banana who?
Knock Knock.
Who's there?
Orange.
Orange who?
Orange you glad I didn't say
banana again?

7. Knock Knock.
Who's there?
Etch.
Etch who?
Bless you!

8. Knock Knock.
Who's there?
Owl.
Owl who?
Yes, they do!

9. Knock Knock.
Who's there?
Tank.
Tank who?
You're welcome!

10. Knock Knock.
Who's there?
Wooden shoe.
Wooden shoe who?
Wooden shoe like to hear another joke?

11. Knock Knock.
Who's there?
Spell.
Spell who?
W-H-O

12.   Knock Knock.
Who's there?
Dishes.
Dishes who?
Dishes a very bad joke.

13.   Knock Knock.
Who's there?
Iva.
Iva who?
I've a sore hand from Knocking!

14.   Knock Knock.
Who's there?
Leaf.
Leaf who?
Leaf me alone!

15.   Knock Knock.
Who's there?
Figs.
Figs who?
Figs the doorbell, it's not working

16. Knock Knock.
Who's there?
Mustache.
Mustache who?
I mustache you a question, but I'll shave it for later.

17. Knock Knock.
Who's there?
Amos.
Amos who?
A mosquito bit me!

18. Knock Knock.
Who's there?
Kanga.
Kanga who?
Actually, it's kangaroo!

19. Knock Knock.
Who's there?
Doris.
Doris who?

Doris locked, that's why I'm Knocking.

20. Knock Knock.
Who's there?
Luke.
Luke who?
Luke through the peephole and find out!

21. Knock Knock.
Who's there?
Yacht.
Yacht who?
Yacht to know me by now!

22. Knock Knock.
Who's there?
Alpaca.
Alpaca who?
Alpaca the trunk, you pack the suitcase!

23. Knock Knock.
Who's there?
Lettuce.
Lettuce who?
Lettuce be friends!

24. Knock Knock.
Who's there?
Dwayne.
Dwayne who?
Dwayne the bathtub, I'm dwowning!

25. Knock Knock.
Who's there?
Cash.
Cash who?
No thanks, I'll have some peanuts.

26. Knock Knock.
Who's there?
Woo.
Woo who?

Don't get too excited, it's just a joke!

27. Knock Knock.
Who's there?
Dozen.
Dozen who?
Dozen anybody want to let me in?

28. Knock Knock.
Who's there?
Interrupting doctor.
Interrupting doc-
YOU NEED A COLONOSCOPY!

29. Knock Knock.
Who's there?
Hatch.
Hatch who? Bless you!

30. Knock Knock.
Who's there?
Dejav.
Dejav who? Knock Knock

31. Knock Knock.
Who's there?
Lettuce.
Lettuce who?
Lettuce in and we'll tell you!

32. Knock Knock.
Who's there?
Annie. Annie who?
Annie thing you can do, I can do better!

33. Knock Knock.
Who's there?
Celine.
Celine who?
Celine a doctor lately? You don't look well!

34. Knock Knock.
Who's there?
Fiona.
Fiona who? Fiona dog, Open the door!

35. Knock Knock.
Who's there?
Goat.
Goat who?
Goat to the door and find out!

36. Knock Knock.
Who's there?
Hawaii.
Hawaii who?
I'm fine, Hawaii you?

37. Knock Knock.
Who's there?
Ida.
Ida who?
Ida like to come in now, please!

38. Knock Knock.
Who's there?
Justin.
Justin who?
Justin time for dinner!

39.   Knock Knock.
Who's there?
Ketchup.
Ketchup who?
Ketchup with me and I'll tell you!

40.   Knock Knock.
Who's there?
Mikey.
Mikey who?
Mikey doesn't fit in the keyhole!

41.   Knock Knock.
Who's there?
Noah.
Noah who?
Noah good place to eat around here?

42.   Knock Knock.
Who's there?
Olive.
Olive who?

Olive you and I don't care who knows it!

43. Knock Knock.
Who's there?
Pizza.
Pizza who?
Pizza cake to make these jokes!

44. Knock Knock.
Who's there?
Quiche.
Quiche who?
Quiche me if you can!

45. Knock Knock.
Who's there?
Robin.
Robin who?
Robin you, so hand over the cash!

46. Knock Knock.
Who's there?
Sadie.

Sadie who?
Sadie magic word and I'll let you in!

47. Knock Knock.
Who's there?
Theodore.
Theodore who?
Theodore wasn't opened so I Knocked!

48. Knock Knock.
Who's there?
Turnip.
Turnip who?
Turnip the volume, it's quiet in here.

49. Knock Knock.
Who's there?
Voodoo.
Voodoo who?
Voodoo you think you are, asking all these questions?

50. Knock Knock.
Who's there?
Wendy.
Wendy who?
Wendy wind dies down, we can go sailing!

51. Knock Knock.
Who's there?
Xavier.
Xavier who?
Xavier breath, it's just a Knock-Knock joke!

52. Knock Knock.
Who's there?
Little old lady.
Little old lady who?
Wow! I didn't know you could yodel!

53. Knock Knock.
Who's there?
Zeke.

Zeke who?
Zeke and ye shall find!

54.   Knock Knock.
Who's there?
Abby.
Abby who?
Abby birthday to you!

55.   Knock Knock.
Who's there?
Bless.
Bless who?
Bless you, did you sneeze?

56.   Knock Knock.
Who's there?
Candice.
Candice who?
Candice door open, or am I stuck out here?

57.   bKnock Knock.
Who's there?

Dewey.
Dewey who?
Dewey have to keep telling these jokes?

58. Knock Knock.
Who's there?
Euripides.
Euripides who?
Euripides clothes, you pay for them!

59. Knock Knock.
Who's there?
Fir.
Fir who?
Fir goodness sake, open the door!

60. Knock Knock.
Who's there?
Gorilla.
Gorilla who?
Gorilla me a hamburger, would you?

61. Knock Knock.
Who's there?
Harry.
Harry who?
Harry up, it's cold out here!

62. Knock Knock.
Who's there?
Juno.
Juno who?
Juno what time it is? My watch stopped.

63. Knock Knock.
Who's there?
Kermit.
Kermit who?
Kermit a crime, and you'll do time!

64. Knock Knock.
Who's there?
Mummy.
Mummy who?

Mummy's the word, I won't tell anyone you're home!

65. Knock Knock.
Who's there?
Nana.
Nana who?
Nana your business who's at the door!

66. Knock Knock.
Who's there?
Oahu.
Oahu who?
Oahu doing? Let me in!

67. Knock Knock.
Who's there?
Pecan.
Pecan who?
Pecan someone your own size!

68. Knock Knock.
Who's there?

Quota.
Quota who?
Quota lot of Knock-Knock jokes do you know?

69.   Knock Knock.
Who's there?
Roach.
Roach who?
Roach you a letter, did you get it?

70.   Knock Knock.
Who's there?
Snow.
Snow who?
Snow use, the door's locked!

Sports

1. Why did the pickleball player bring a pickle jar to the game?
He wanted to serve up some dill-icious shots!

2. What do you call a pickleball player who's always making mistakes?
A dink-a-link.

3. Why do pickleball players have so many friends?
They always keep a good "net"-work!

4. What do you say to a hot pickleball player who is mad?
Take a Chill Dill!

5. Who is Ben Johns always on the phone with: Callin' Johns

6. What do you call a pickleball player who's always cold? A chilly dink.

7. Why did the pickleball player bring a ladder to the game? To work on his overhead smash!

8. What do you call it when a pickleball player is always taking their time? They are always dinking around

9. Why did pickleball player bring a whole pizza to the game?
To work on his Slice.

10. Why is Ben Johns always on the phone?
Because he's callin' Johns.

11. Which pro pickleball player loves sandwiches?
Jimmy John's.

12. What do you call it when the pickleball player was making Sushi on the back side of the paddle?
Back-Hand-Roll

13. What is it called when a pickleball player has a problem?
A Dill-lema.

14. Why are bangers always thirsty?
Because they don't know how to dink.

15. What do you call A Pickleball player that gets pickled?
Sour.

16. Why are pickleball players so happy all the time?
The game is so Dill-lightfull!.

17. What do you call a pickleball player who's always changing their mind?
A flip-flopper.

18. Why did the basketball player bring a ladder to the game?
He wanted to get high scores!

19. What do you call a monkey that plays basketball?
A chimp off the old block.

20. Why don't basketball players go on vacation?

They'd rather stay in their own court.

21. What do you call a basketball player who sweats a lot?
A dribbler.

22. Why was the basketball court wet?
The players kept dribbling all over it.

23. Why don't football players ever sweat?
They have good fans!

24. Why couldn't the football coach play cards?

Because he kept losing his quarterback.

25. Why did the football coach go to the bank?
To get his quarter back.

26. What do you call the funniest part of a football joke?
The punt-line!

27. What do you call a wizard who is bad at football?
Fumbledore.

28. What do you call a football player who's always in a bad mood?
A gridiron.

29. What do you call a football player who's always cold?
A tight end.

30. Why don't football players ever get hot?
They're surrounded by fans.

31. Why did the football player bring string to the game?
He wanted to tie the score.

32. Why did Cinderella get kicked off the football team?

Because she kept running away from the ball!

33. What tea do soccer players drink?
Penal-tea!

34. What do you call a soccer player wearing headphones?
Deaf-ender!

35. Why did the soccer player take up acting?
He was good at playing the field.

36. What do you call a soccer player who's always borrowing money?

A loan striker.

37. Why don't famous soccer players ever get hot?
They have plenty of fans.

38. Why don't grasshoppers watch football?
They prefer cricket!

39. Why did the soccer ball quit the team?
It was tired of being kicked around!

40. What do you call a monkey that plays basketball?
A chimp off the old block.

41.   Why don't
basketball players
go on vacation?
They'd rather stay
in their own court.

42.   What do you call a
basketball player
who only scores
three-pointers?
A three-peat
offender.

43.   What do you call a
cat that plays
basketball?
A furward.

44.   What part of a
football pitch
smells nicest?
The scenter spot!

45. What do you call a basketball player on a minefield?
Kobe!

46. Why did the golfer bring two pairs of pants?
In case he got a hole in one.

47. What do you call a boomerang that doesn't come back?
A stick.

48. Why don't scientists trust atoms?
Because they make up everything, even in sports!

49. Why did the cantaloupe jump into the pool?
It wanted to become a watermelon!

50. Why did Cinderella get kicked off the baseball team?
She always ran away from the ball.

51. Why did the gym close down?
It just didn't work out.

52. What do you call a pickleball player who's always smiling?
A dill-lightful competitor!

53. Why don't skeletons play basketball?
They don't have the guts.

54. What did the pickle say when it scored a point in pickleball?
"I relish this moment!"

55. How does a pickleball player stay cool during a game?
They always serve with a dill!

56. Why was the baseball team so good at math?

They knew how to count on each other!

57. Why don't basketball players ever go on vacation?
They're afraid of traveling!

58. Why did the pickleball player bring a ladder to the match?
To reach new heights in their game!

59. Why was the baseball player a great musician?
He had perfect pitch!

60. How do pickleball players keep their spirits high during a tough match? They keep things "pickle"-tively positive!

61. Why are bangers always thirsty? Because they don't know how to dink.

62. A Pickleball player that gets pickled? Sour

Animal Antics

1. What do you call a bear with no teeth?
A gummy bear!

2. Why don't oysters donate to charity?
Because they're shellfish!

3. What do you call a sleeping bull?
A bulldozer!

4. How do you make an octopus laugh?
With ten-tickles!

5. Why don't ants get sick?
Because they have tiny ant-ibodies!

6. What do you call a pig that does karate?
A pork chop!

7. Why can't a leopard hide?
Because he's always spotted!

8. What do you get when you cross a snowman with a vampire?
Frostbite!

9. Why don't eggs tell jokes?
They'd crack each other up!

10. What do you call a fly without wings?
A walk!

11. Why are fish so smart?
Because they live in schools!

12. What do you call a bear with no ears?
B!

13. Why don't sharks eat clowns?
Because they taste funny!

14. What do you call a sleeping dinosaur?
A dino-snore!

15. Why did the duck get arrested?
For selling quack!

16. What do you call a dog magician?
A labracadabrador!

17. Why don't crabs give to charity?

Because they're shellfish!

18. What do you call a cat that's been caught by the police?
The purrpetrator!

19. Why did the chicken join a band?
Because it had the drumsticks!

20. What do you call a rabbit with fleas?
Bugs Bunny!

21. Why did the frog call his insurance company?
He had a jump in his car!

22. What do you call a penguin in the Sahara desert?
Lost!

23. Why don't moths watch football on TV?
They prefer the radio because they eat clothes!

24. How do you catch a squirrel?
Climb a tree and act like a nut!

25. What do you call a wolf with a cold?
A-choo!

26. Why don't snakes wear shoes?
Because they can't tie their laces!

27. What do you call a monkey with a banana in each ear?
Anything you want, it can't hear you!

28. How do you make a goldfish old?
Take away the 'g'!

29. What do you call a deer with no eyes?
No eye deer!

30. Why don't elephants use computers?
They're afraid of the mouse!

31. What do you get when you cross a snake with a pie?
A python!

32. How do you know if there's an elephant under your bed?
Your nose touches the ceiling!

33. What do you call a bear caught in the rain?
A drizzly bear!

34. Why don't oysters share their pearls?
They're shellfish!

35. What do you call a cow on a dryer?
A milkshake!

36. How do snails fight?
They slug it out!

37. What kind of dog can jump higher than a building?
A dog—buildings can't jump!

38. Why can't a leopard play hide and seek?
Because he's always spotted!

39. What do you call a fly without wings?
A walk!

40. Why don't sharks eat clowns?
Because they taste funny!

41. What do you call a sleeping cow?
A bull-dozer!

42. Why are flamingos so flexible?
They're pretty in pink!

43. What do you call a cat that swallows a duck?
A duck-filled-fatty-puss!

44. What do you call a horse that lives next door?
A neigh-bor!

45. Why did the cow cross the road?
To get to the udder side!

46. How do you make a slow dog fast?
Take away its food bowl!

Food

1. What do you call a fake noodle?
An impasta!

2. How do eggs stay fit?
They egg-cercise!

3. What do you call an obvious banana?
DUH-nana.

4. What do you call an egg that goes on safari?
An eggs-plorer!

5. What did the egg do when it saw the frying pan?
It scrambled!

6. Why did the cookie go to the doctor?
Because it was feeling crumbly.

7. Why did the tomato blush?
Because it saw the salad dressing!

8. Why don't eggs tell jokes?
They'd crack each other up.

9. What do you call cheese that isn't yours?
Nacho cheese!

10. Why did the grape stop in the middle of the road?
Because he ran out of juice.

11. What did the grape say when it got stepped on?
Nothing, it just let out a little wine.

12. Why did the peanut butter go to the doctor?
It wasn't feeling very smooth.

13. Why did the lettuce win the race?
Because it was ahead.

14. Why did the cookie go to the nurse?
Because it was feeling crumbly.

15. Why did the bread roll away?
Because it saw the butter knife.

16. What did the Egg get on the test?
An E for Egg-cellent.

17. Why did the bacon laugh?
Because it was egg-cited.

18. Why do cheeses never worry about anything?
Because everything's gonna brie all right.

19. Why did the yogurt go to the art exhibit?
Because it was cultured.

20. Why did the garlic go to the dance?
To get a little spice in its life.

21. What do you call a group of berries playing instruments?
A jam session.

22. I'm on a seafood diet.
I see food and I eat it.

23. Why did the coffee file a police report?
It got mugged.

24. What kind of room doesn't have doors?
A mushroom!

25. What did the man stare at the orange juice?
Because it said concentrate.

26. Why don't melons get married?
Because they cantaloupe!

27. Why did the banana go to the doctor?
It wasn't peeling well.

28. Why was the cheese looking so down?

It was feeling blue.

29. What do you call a fake potato?
An imitator!

30. Why did the flour go to the doctor?
It was feeling a bit kneady.

31. What do you call a lazy pepper?
A bell-dropper.

32. What do you call a fruit that's always complaining?
Its not a fruit anymore - just a wine.

33. What do you call a sad lemon?
A sour puss.

34. Why did the pickle blush?
Because it saw the salad undressing.

35. Why did the onion win an award?
It really brought tears to everyone's eyes.

36. What do you call a vegetable that's good at boxing?
A brussel sprout.

37. What do you call a smart fruit?
A brain-ana.

38. What do you call a cow on a trampoline?
A milk shake!

39. What do you call a vegetable that tells fibs?
A fibber bean.

40. Why did the mushroom go to the party?
Because he was a fun guy.

41. Why did the cookie go to the party?
He was feeling chip-per!

42. Why did the cookie file a police report?
It got wafer-ed.

43. What did the grape say when it got stepped on?
Nothing, it just let out a little wine.

Pun-tastic Puns

1. What is the healthiest way for Mom to roll her eyes?
Spiralies!

2. Why don't eggs tell jokes?
They'd crack each other up!

3. I'm reading a book about anti-gravity.
It's impossible to put down!

4. Why do cows have hooves instead of feet?
Because they lactose.

5. What do you call a can opener that doesn't work?
A can't opener!

6. Why did the scarecrow win an award?
He was outstanding in his field.

7. Why don't scientists trust atoms?
Because they make up everything.

8. What do you call a parade of rabbits hopping backwards?
A receding hare-line.

9. Why did the math book look so sad?
Because it had too many problems!

10. What do you call a boomerang that doesn't come back?
A stick.

11. Why don't skeletons fight each other?
They don't have the guts.

12. Why did the bicycle fall over?
Because it was two-tired.

13. How do you organize a space party?
You planet.

14. Why don't bacteria tell each other secrets?
Because they might spread.

15. Why did the gym close down?
It just didn't work out...

16. What do you call a factory that makes okay products?
A satisfactory.

17. Why did the invisible man turn down the job offer?
He couldn't see himself doing it.

18. What do you call your banana-loving grandmother?
Ba-Nana!

19. Why don't melons get married?
Because they cantaloupe.

20. What do you call a cheese that isn't yours?

Nacho cheese!

21. What do you call a fake fish?
A phony fillet.

22. What do you call a smart fruit?
A brain-ana.

23. Why did the yogurt go to the art exhibit?
Because it was cultured.

Miscellaneous Mischief

1. I'm reading a book about anti-gravity.
It's impossible to put down!

2. Why did the gym close down?
It just didn't work out...

3. What do you call a factory that makes okay products?
A satisfactory.

4. Why did the cookie file a police report?
It got wafered.

5. What do you call a cow with no legs?
Ground beef.

6. What's a tornado's favorite game?

Twister!

7. How do you make a tissue dance?
   Put a little boogie in it.

8. Why did the computer go to the doctor?
   It had a virus.

9. Why was the broom late?
   It swept in.

10. Why do skeletons have low self-esteem?
    They have no body to love.

11. How does a penguin build its house?
    Igloos it together!

12. Why doesn't Batman go to church?
He has issues with Robin.

13. What's Superman's favorite snack?
Krypto-nite!

14. Why did Wonder Woman fail her driving test?
She couldn't find her invisible car.

15. How does Aquaman cut his hair?
With a sea-saw!

16. What's Thor's favorite day of the week?
Thorsday!

17. Why doesn't the Hulk use Twitter?

He prefers to Smash-tag.

18. What's Aquaman's favorite type of music?
Swim-phony.

19. How does Iron Man keep his suit shiny?
With metal polish.

20. Why did Spider-Man get kicked out of the library?
He kept getting caught in the world wide web.

21. What's Spider-Man's favorite day of the week?
Web-nesday.

22. What do you call Spider-Man's brother?

Peter Parkour.

23. Why did Batman's girlfriend break up with him?
She couldn't handle his emotional baggage.

24. Why did Batman's mother call him for dinner?
"Dinner, dinner, dinner, dinner, Batman!"

25. What do you call Chewbacca when he gets chocolate in his fur?
A Chocolate Chip Wookiee.

26. Why did Anakin Skywalker cross the road?
To get to the Dark Side.

27. How does Darth Vader like his toast?
On the dark side.

28. Why did Wonder Woman get into trouble at school?
She couldn't find her invisible homework!

29. Why didn't the toilet paper cross the road?
Because it got stuck in a crack!

30. Why couldn't the chicken lay an egg?
Buckaws!

31. Why did the kid cross the road?
To get to the other slide.

32. Couldn't the cat cross the road?
Because it was afraid -y- cat.

33. Why do you need to be careful around stairs?
Because they're always up to something.

www.ingramcontent.com/pod-product-compliance
Lightning Source LLC
LaVergne TN
LVHW061621070526
838199LV00078B/7368